#GOOGLE+ for BUSINESS **tweet** Book01

Put the Power of Google+ to Work for Your Business

By Janet Fouts

Foreword by Steve Farnsworth

E-mail: info@thinkaha.com
20660 Stevens Creek Blvd., Suite 210
Cupertino, CA 95014

Published by *THiNKaha*®, a Happy About® imprint
20660 Stevens Creek Blvd., Suite 210, Cupertino, CA 95014
http://thinkaha.com

First Printing: March 2012
Paperback ISBN: 978-1-61699-072-5 (1-61699-072-4)
eBook ISBN: 978-1-61699-073-2 (1-61699-073-2)
Place of Publication: Silicon Valley, California, USA
Paperback Library of Congress Number: 2011939881

Advance Praise

"A helpful and thought-provoking primer on using Google+!"
Jason Alba, Author, *I'm on LinkedIn—Now What???*

"In today's fast-paced social media environment, it can be hard to determine which platforms will bring value without logging countless hours trying to figure them out. This book quickly answers some of the important questions to guide your thinking on the benefits of Google+."
Angela Connor (*@communitygirl*), VP, Director of Social Media, Capstrat, Author, *18 Rules of Community Engagement*

"One of those rare books on a new social media platform that is both packed with practical information that you can use immediately, but is a joy to read, too."
Steve Farnsworth (*@Steveology*), Chief Digital Marketing Officer, Jolt Social Media

"Google+ is possibly the only place available online that successfully blends social networking, great collaboration tools, and a bevy of ways to find people and information that interest you. Janet provides bite-sized tips and advice to help you get the most from using Google+. Whether you're a large brand or a solo entrepreneur, Google+ should be on your radar and in your web browser."
Adam Helweh, Principal & Founder, Secret Sushi Creative – Deliciously Creative Design & Marketing

"If you've been holding back from Google+, take heart—Janet will steer you through the Google+ jungle with this very readable, engaging, and surprisingly comprehensive guide."
Mark Ivey, Partner, The ION Group

"In the sea of social media confusion, comes a practical guide that answers not only 'why' we should set up a Google+ page, but 'how' we should then engage with it—all in consumable bites of actionable advice."
Jim Joseph, President, Cohn & Wolfe North America, Author, *The Experience Effect for Small Business*, Professor, New York University

"Janet Fouts has created a useful handbook for using Google+ to charge your business. Google+ is fast becoming a must-have in the world of online community, and Janet shows you how to use it to the best advantage for your business. A great read for any business owner who wants to build a successful online community."
Miranda Marquit, Co-author, *Community 101: How to Grow an Online Community*

"*#GOOGLE+ for BUSINESS tweet* is a quick read yet provides compelling insight into this new community called GOOGLE+. As proficient as I am, Janet provided observations I hadn't thought of in my own experience. Now that does #RockTheWorld!"
Lori Ruff (*@LoriRuff, @LinkedInDiva*), Social Media Speaker, Trainer, Author & Host

"If you ever wanted to start using Google+ for your business, a great starter book for you is Janet Fout's *#GOOGLE+ for BUSINESS tweet*. The author has distilled the most important information you need to know in the form of tweets. It's easy to read and simple to understand. Highly recommended."
Kiruba Shankar, CEO, Business Blogging, Co-author, *#CROWDSOURCING tweet*

"*#GOOGLE+ for BUSINESS tweet* spells out in sweet and simple terms what you need to get your business started on Google+. Read it from start to finish, or just pick out a few 'tweets' a day and you'll have all you need to get tip after tip to get your business going on Google+."
Jesse Stay, Author, *Google+ For Dummies, I'm on Facebook—Now What???*

Dedication

To CJ and Mike.

No matter how crazy my life gets, they keep me grounded and support me in all my endeavors.

Thank you, thank you.

Janet Fouts

Acknowledgments

To my publisher, Mitchell Levy, who urges me on when a new topic evolves into a book; THiNKaha's Production Manager, Diane Vo, who kept me on track and made the book the best it could be. A special shout-out to all the wonderful people I've met using Google+ and the fantastic development team behind the scenes who are constantly checking in with the users and modifying to make this social network really work for the people who use it.

Janet Fouts

Why I Wrote This Book

Google+ pulled together some of the best elements of my favorite social media networks. Initially, there's been a lot of angst from small business about learning "another social media network," but I maintain that it's going to be a critical network for business. I hope that the reader finds inspiration to give Google+ a try and an understanding of how to use it to build their brand in Google's massive empire through these 140 tweet-length tips.

If you want to learn more about how to use Google+ for business or building your personal brand—or you need training for your staff—connect with me!

Janet Fouts

Google+: http://gplus.to/jfouts

Twitter: http://twitter.com/jfouts

LinkedIn: http://linkedin.com/in/janetfouts

Facebook: http://facebook.com/jfouts

Blog: http://janetfouts.com

Email: janet@janetfouts.com

How to Read a THiNKaha® Book
A Note from the Publisher

The THiNKaha series is the CliffsNotes of the 21st century. The value of these books is that they are contextual in nature. Although the actual words won't change, their meaning will change every time you read one as your context will change. Here's how to read one of these books and have it work for you.

1. Read a THiNKaha book (these slim and handy books should only take approximately 15–20 minutes of your time!) and write down one to three "aha" moments you had whilst reading it.

   a. "Aha" moments are looked at as "actionable" moments—think of a specific project you're working on, an event, a sales deal, a personal issue, etc. and see how the ahas in this book can inspire your own "aha!" moment, something that you can specifically act on.

2. Mark your calendar to re-read this book again in 30 days.

3. Repeat step #1 and write down one to three "aha" moments that grab you this time. I guarantee that they will be different than the first time.

After reading a THiNKaha book, writing down your "aha" moments, re-reading it, and writing down more "aha" moments, you'll begin to see how these books contextually apply to you. THiNKaha books advocate for continuous, life-long learning. They will help you transform your "aha" moments into actionable items with tangible results until you no longer have to say "aha!" to these moments—they'll become part of your daily practice as you continue to grow and learn.

As CEO of THiNKaha, I definitely practice what I preach. I read *#CORPORATE CULTURE tweet*, *#LEADERSHIP tweet*, and *#TEAMWORK tweet* once a month and take away two to three different action items from each of them every time. Please e-mail me your "aha" moments.

Mitchell Levy, CEO
publisher@thinkaha.com

Put the Power of Google+ to Work for Your Business

Contents

Foreword by Steve Farnsworth

No matter what the title and focus of the social media workshop or webinar I am giving, it is very common to have someone raise their hand during the Q&A and meekly ask, "Should I have a Facebook page (or Twitter account)?" Now you can add, "Should I have a Google+ profile?" to that list.

I am not alone in getting this common question. Other social media speakers joke among themselves about the regularity of being asked. The part that makes us laugh the most? Our usual answer is, "It depends." Not very smart for people who are supposed to be experts on this stuff.

While it seems like a simple question that any "real" expert should be able to answer, it is a tough question because there are a number of questions that must be answered first.

What do you want to accomplish on that platform? Are your customers already there? What value will you bring to that conversation? Are your goals realistic, and are the results worth your time and resources? The questions go on and on.

But without understanding the platform basics it is hard to answer those questions. Now that Google+ has entered the social media fray, another question people are asking is, "Where should I start?"

If only there was a book for the newest big social media player since Facebook or Twitter. One that let you chose how many bite-sized chunks of insight and tips you consumed in any reading. With the cavalcade of social platforms coming and going, it is hard to get the best information to both let you wrap your head around Google+ and allow you to grasp the basics.

Janet Fouts, an incredibly savvy and sharp digital marketing strategist, understands the need for hands-on and practical advice. She has gathered a first-rate selection of inside information, and distilled each to their core idea.

If you are a business owner who has limited time, a professional who is concerned about personal branding, or someone who wants to stay current on the latest social media, this concise tome is the ideal place to start your Google+ journey.

~ **Steve Farnsworth**

(@Steveology)

Chief Marketing Officer, Jolt Social Media

Section 1

Do I Really Need Google+?

Is Google+ really a good fit for your business and the way you market it online?

1

Google+ is a great choice if you have a well established social media network already and can bring that network with you to Google+.

2

It's probably not a good choice if you've never used other networks. Google+ is not very intuitive to use yet.

3

Are you a thought leader in your industry? Build some circles[1] to share with and create your own personal platform to speak to a whole new audience.

_____

1. See Section IV: Circles.

4

Overwhelmed with social networks? Google+ circles allow you to focus your message to people interested in just that topic.

5

Do you expect instant celebrity status and thousands of followers? You have to earn status on Google+ by sharing real, engaging content.

6

Are you considered a font of useful knowledge amongst your peers? Google+ is a perfect place for you to share that knowledge.

7

Before you start a page for your business, start a personal profile and get comfortable with it before you build a business page.[2]

_____

2. See Section V: Business Pages.

8

If you care about search engine optimization (SEO) for your brand, you should at least have a Google profile, even if you don't use Google+.

9

Google+ is about engaging other people, not broadcasting how wonderful you are. Think more about your audience than yourself.

10

If you read 50 RSS feeds a day and have great information to share, Google+ is a great network to share and discover new sources.

11

If you aren't able to keep the content flowing, stick with a Google profile page that leads people to connect with you.

Section II

Your Profile

Your first step should be to create a complete and interesting profile page. This is your most important page on Google+ and it is how people will get an idea of who you are and why they should follow you.

12

Add as many of your **active** social media profiles as possible. Make it easy for people to learn about you.

13

Put only information you would share with anyone on your profile. No home address, birth date, or anything a scammer could use against you.

14

Use a friendly, inviting picture as your profile image, not a logo. Give people an idea as to why they want to connect with you.

15

Add pictures and video to your profile to tell a story about you and what you are interested in.

16

Change profile pictures periodically and people will re-visit your profile page more often.

17

Be sure to add links to your website, blog, and other social media networks to help people find you.

18

Your profile will be where people get the best idea of who you are. Read it from a new visitor's perspective. What do you think of you?

19

When you click a +1 button on someone else's profile, it's a vote of support for them. Think of it as a virtual pat on the back.

20

When someone +1s your
post, reciprocate by +1ing
something they say or
sharing one of their posts. It's
a way of saying thank you.

21

Monitor your settings page carefully to control who sees your circles, your posts, who can chat with you, and who can send you messages.

22

Transparency is crucial. If you are working for a company and comment on their posts, say so—either on the post or in your profile.

23

Remember that only your publicly shared posts show up on your profile. Share posts that will encourage new follows.

24

Users can see your tagline when they mouse over your name on posts—make yours descriptive and unique.

25

Be sure to link your profile to other sites that are about you. These links will show up in search results as authored by you.

26

Add the meta tag *rel= "author"* to your personal sites and blog for optimal SEO for your personal brand.

Section III

Getting Started

This section has all the nuts and bolts you'll need to use Google+ with the best of 'em.

27

Read the "Stream" link under your profile to see what the people you have circled are talking about.

28

Vary your content. Pictures and videos are shared the most but you must have something to say, too...don't you? Express yourself.

29

See if someone is following you and who they are following by visiting their profile, then decide if you want to circle them.

30

If you don't want your content re-shared, don't put it online. "Disable re-share" isn't protection from a simple cut and paste.

31

Do some searches to find others talking about what you want to talk about. Create circles that reflect the topic as well as the person.

32

If you see a new post with just a few comments, NOW is the time to jump in with your own—don't wait. The early comment gets more views.

33

Press the "Enter" key to open up the comments and view all of them before you add a comment to avoid duplicates.

34

Comments add value and turn a post into a conversation. Click "Reply to Author" to include them in your comment and so they are notified.

35

Press the space bar to scroll down the stream you are viewing.

36

You can chat[3] directly from the stream. Why not start a chat on the fly over a hot topic?

---

3. See Section VI: Hangouts and Chat.

37

To mention a person or business in a post, type +username (i.e. +Janet Fouts); as you type, Google+ will offer options to select.

38

Click the timestamp on a post to get a permalink to share on other social networks and invite them to the party.

39

"Sparks" are topics you can use as a starting point to share good information. Follow your favorite hot topics.

40

Sparks help Google get a better idea of what interests you and to potentially suggest you as a follow to someone with similar interests.

41

Do a search to find interesting information in your niche and create some Sparks specific to your interests.

42

Create Sparks for your business and your own name to follow what is being said about you.

43

To mute a post that is getting a lot of comments, click the arrow in the top right of the post and "mute post".

44

You can geo-locate your posts if you wish to tell people where you are when you post.

45

Share a post privately with an individual by typing +username (i.e. +Janet Fouts) and sharing only with them (not with circles).

46

Find influencers and frequent sharers by clicking the "Ripples" on a post to see who else is sharing or +1ing that post. Circle them.

47

Use Ripples to find good
sharers (who are also
frequently shared) to add to
your own circles.

48

Post at least 3-4 times per day to make sure you are seen by your followers, but make sure it is relevant to your audience.

49

Pay attention to what information gets the most re-shares and comments. Fine tune your messaging to what your followers want to hear about.

50

Commenting on the post of
an influencer & adding value
to their post is great, but don't
add a "Me too!" just to get
seen in their stream.

Section IV

Circles

Google circles are a cute name for groups. When you start to create connections on Google+, you are encouraged to group them into circles so you can sort people by what they are interested in and what you would like to share with them.

51

Circles are like follows on Twitter. You can follow someone and they don't have to follow you back.

52

You can have as many circles as you want but try to be organized or they could get away from you!

53

Search for "shared circles" to find entire groups of people interested in the same things you are. Grab the whole circle or a few.

54

If you add someone to both a private circle and a public one, people will see you are following them.

55

The point of circles is to share with people who are interested in that topic. Don't over-share irrelevant information with your circles.

56

Add someone to a circle by clicking the "Add to Circles" button. Then select 1 or more circles to add them to from the menu.

57

Remove someone from a circle by viewing the circle in a tab and then drag them out of the circle. If they are in other circles, repeat.

58

When people are added to a circle they get an email letting them know. Have something to interest them when they view your profile.

59

Click on the name of a circle and it shows the posts of only the people in that circle.

60

Create circles around your interests, to sort business connections by topic, for people who share non-work information, for family.

61

Make circles of people you can learn from or would like to know better. Visit the stream of those circles often to create new relationships.

62

Bookmark items for future reading by creating a circle with no one in it. Share items there as bookmarks for future reading or sharing.

63

Share with your circles respectfully. Share what you know will interest them to encourage them to add you to circles.

64

Share circles by viewing a circle and then click "Share This Circle" in the upper right corner of the page.

65

If you share a circle it lets everyone in that circle know who they were circled with and the name of the circle.

66

Move someone from one circle to another by dragging them from circle to circle.

67

Turn negative comments into opportunities to discuss and correct misconceptions. Don't delete comments unless they are offensive.

68

Commenting on someone's post with a link to your own information on another topic is spam.

69

Commenting on another person's post with additional information that is relevant or your own perspective is the way to go.

70

Remember that your public posts show up in Google search. What do you want people to see there?

Section V

Business Pages

The idea with business pages on Google+ is clearly to compete with Facebook fan pages and for some businesses it may be a better fit. That said, there is plenty of room in the market for both social networks. It really depends on how you communicate best with your market.

71

Google+ pages help people see your business as "the one who knows everything" by simply sharing great, relevant information publicly.

72

Pages can't +1 other pages or on a website.

73

The default setting for posting on a page is public.

74

Let people know about your business page with a badge on your website.

75

Business pages can't add people to their circles until the person circles them first.

76

Unlike profiles, business pages do not receive notifications via email, text, or in the Google bar.

77

Google+ pages un-circle you automatically if you un-circle them.

78

Business pages can't send messages to other pages until they have circled them.

79

With business pages it's even more important to share public posts there than to circles so people find the posts and circle the page.

80

Google+ pages can't send you information or even mention you until you have circled them.

81

Even if you haven't circled someone, if they have circled your page, your posts show up in their public stream.

82

Find Google+ pages for big brands or companies by typing in +brandname (i.e. +Dell for Dell computers) in the Google search engine.

83

+1 a business page to show your support for what they do and to learn more about their business, and to receive messages from them.

84

Make a habit of sharing on your business page and encourage staff to share the posts on the page with their own networks.

85

Make sure people know about your page. Put it on your website, in your email signature, tweet it, and send out an email announcement!

86

Remind your Google+ friends about your business page often to encourage it to grow. Send out links to useful info you've posted there.

87

Business pages can circle other business pages. How about creating circles to share within your industry?

88

In the "Category" tab, add categories to your local business page to help users better understand what your business does.

89

Add categories to your local business page to help people understand what you do.

90

Google+ Direct Connect creates a direct link to your brand page when someone types a +brandname (i.e. +Your Brand) in Google search.

91

A page's eligibility for Direct Connect is based on relevancy and popularity. You must connect your website and Google+ to be considered.

92

You can set Google+ to automatically add brand pages to your page circles when you search for that brand in the page settings tab.

93

You can add multiple admins to a business page. Select carefully—they hold your brand in their hands.

Section VI

Hangouts and Chat

Hangouts are live video chats
between individuals or groups.
All you need to participate is a
webcam and a microphone.

94

Before you do a hangout for your business, test it with friends to make sure all works well.

95

Hangouts work with Google Translate so multi-language communication can happen almost instantly.

96

Create a hangout and record it to share on your blog or website. Let people know they are being recorded.

97

Google keeps a log of who was in the hangout with you. Follow up with an email or message.

98

View the profiles of people in a hangout and add them to circles or at least thank them for hanging out.

99

Use the chat fields in the hangout to chat with other users participating in the hangout.

100

Set up a live video feed with a remote team to introduce them to one another.

101

Offer "office hours" for your
customers to come online
and chat with you and
your team.

102

Use hangouts between two classrooms to discuss topics they are covering in class or to introduce other cultures.

103

Teach staff new procedures and policies in a hangout and follow it with a quiz.

104

Hold a weekly hangout newscast for news in your industry. Regular scheduling gives people something to look forward to and more interaction.

105

Leverage your global access.
Learn Spanish in a hangout with a
teacher in Spain.

106

Use hangouts to collaborate on a
project in real time, even share a video
and discuss during the hangout.

107

Teach impromptu cooking classes from your own kitchen and invite friends to share their own recipes.

108

Host a virtual wine tasting with friends around the world. Open your bottles at once and share your review in real time.

109

Capture your hangout with a screen capture tool like Camtasia or Screenflow.

110

Create a hangout for a team meeting and share documents live through Google Docs.

111

Interview a potential employee in a hangout.

112

Users must be invited to chat and accept in order to be added to your chat list.

113

Users who have access to your chat will also gain access to your Gmail address.

114

You can start a Google chat on your mobile phone; the conversation will be on Google+, too, when you log in.

115

Pseudonyms are not allowed in Google+ Chat. Google will send you one warning to change your name before suspending.

116

When you invite someone to chat, a green dot will show next to their name under the chat window to indicate they accepted.

117

If you don't see someone you want to chat with in the chat list, start typing their name into the search box.

118

Unlike with hangouts, people must be in your circles in order to start a chat with them.

119

Google Chat will show anyone you have chatted with in Gmail, Orkut, iGoogle, and many other third party apps.

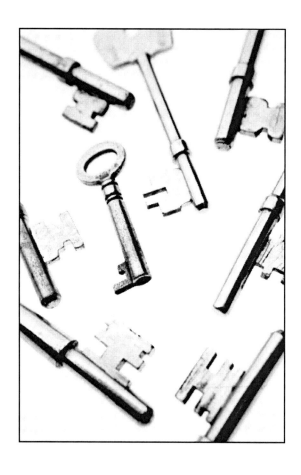

Section VII

Strategy for Success

The tips in this section are going to help you make the most of using Google+ for business.

120

Define your goals for using Google+
and keep your focus on those goals.

121

Create an editorial calendar so you can
see the general messaging you want
to send out on Google+ combined with
other networks.

122

Sharing fresh content that hasn't been shared yet will get you many more shares than posts that have been shared already.

123

Be the first to comment or share on fresh content in order to gain regular followers.

124

Reciprocity is important. If someone consistently shares your posts, look to see how you can support them back.

125

Look at the Ripples of the conversations around you. Who shares the most interesting, relevant content? Share them.

126

An influencer is someone who is frequently shared, +1ed, or whose posts are frequently commented on.

127

Find the influencers in your network and get to know what they like to share. Talk to them regularly and share great information.

128

Set alerts for when someone comments on your posts. Respond as quickly as you can, keep the conversation going.

129

Search outside of Google+ for content people haven't already seen.

130

If you post something that is older material, add a new twist to it with a personal viewpoint.

131

Questions are good. Ask leading questions to start a discussion.

132

Leave open-ended questions so people have something to respond to.

133

When posting a link to an article, add your own take on the subject, not just the title of the article.

134

Curate specific information to send to each of your circles. People respond well to thoughtfully curated material.

135

Be the center of the topic by being the one who finds the best resources in that category.

136

Be consistent with the timing of your posts. If people know you post every morning at 10, they'll start to look forward to your posts.

137

Look for new people to connect with instead of the usual suspects everyone else is following.

138

Create a circle of businesspeople in your industry to do hangouts with and talk about the future of the business.

139

Remember that a conversation online may only result in a sale when you connect offline. Follow up.

140

Think SEO when you make public posts. What do you want people to associate your profile with? It's your brand identity.

Appendix A: Keyboard Shortcuts and Tips to Using Google+

Keyboard Shortcuts

Here are a few basic shortcut keys while in Google+.

- Q: open chat
- K: scroll up within a single post
- J: scroll down within a single post
- Return or Enter: start a comment
- Tab and Return: end a comment
- Space bar: scroll down your stream

Some Basic Tips to Using Google+

- Mention or tag other users or pages with either a + or @ before their name (i.e. +Janet Fouts or @Janet Fouts). Google+ will auto-fill as you type.
- View how your profile looks to a particular user by entering their name in the search box—you can then see how your profile looks from their account.
- To share a photo, drag the URL of the image into your post.
- Google allows photos to be edited with their built-in photo editor. Click "Edit Photo" in the "Actions" menu.
- If your mouse has a mouse wheel, you can use it to easily scroll through photos.

Managing a Google+ Page

If you receive an invitation to manage a Google+ page, click the provided link in the invitation and it will take you to a log-in screen.

You will need a Gmail account to log in with (you should create a profile so they know who you are). Log into Gmail and they'll take you to another screen where you will accept the "Terms of Use" and *poof* you're a manager!

Once you become a manager for a page, you'll see a blue box in the upper left corner that says "Manage this Page". You will see the page stream and you'll be able to create and manage circles and follows just as though you own the page.

Adding Managers

Figure 1

As the owner of the page, log in and select the page you want to manage. Select the little gear in the upper right corner of the page and go to "Google+ settings" (Figure 1). You'll see an option for managers on the left side of the page (Figure 2).

Figure 2

Invite a new manager by entering their email; Google will send them an email inviting them to manage your page.

You can have as many as 50 managers per page.

If you change your mind and want to take back an invitation before it is accepted, just click the "x" next to their name on the managers list.

The owner's and manager's name are only seen on the management tab. They are not visible to visitors to the page.

Removing Managers

Removing managers is just as easy as adding them. Go to the "Google+ settings" link for the page you want to remove your managers from and click "Managers" on the left-hand side menu. Click the small "x" to the right of the manager's name and they will be removed from managing the page. Both the manager and the page owner will be notified of who removed them.

Transferring Ownership

Go to the "Managers" page in your "Google+ settings" and click "Transfer Ownership". Select the manager you want to transfer ownership to and confirm the transfer. When an owner transfers the ownership of the page, the previous owner becomes a manager by default.

Click the "Settings" link and go to the "Managers" page. You'll need to make the new owner a manager and they must accept before this next step.

About the Author

Janet Fouts is an acclaimed social media coach, author, speaker, and entrepreneur. She works with a variety of businesses around the world to understand social media for business. Her books, Social Media Success!, *#SOCIALMEDIA PR tweet*, and *#SOCIALMEDIA NONPROFIT tweet*, draw on over 15 years of experience in online marketing and social media, working in the trenches with businesses of all sizes. In addition to her social media coaching practice (http://www.janetfouts.com), Janet is Founder of the Social Media Coaching Center and Senior Partner at Tatu Digital Media, a San Jose inbound marketing and website development agency.

Other Books in the THiNKaha Series

The THiNKaha book series is for thinking adults who lack the time or desire to read long books, but want to improve themselves with knowledge of the most up-to-date subjects. THiNKaha is a leader in timely, cutting-edge books and mobile applications from relevant experts that provide valuable information in a fun, Twitter-brief format for a fast-paced world.

They are available online at http://thinkaha.com or at other online and physical bookstores.

1. *#BOOK TITLE tweet Book01:* 140 Bite-Sized Ideas for Compelling Article, Book, and Event Titles by Roger C. Parker

2. *#BUSINESS SAVVY PM tweet Book01:* Project Management Mindsets, Skills, and Tools for Generating Successful Business Results by Cinda Voegtli

3. *#COACHING tweet Book01:* 140 Bite-Sized Insights On Making A Difference Through Executive Coaching by Sterling Lanier

4. *#CONTENT MARKETING tweet Book01:* 140 Bite-Sized Ideas to Create and Market Compelling Content by Ambal Balakrishnan

5. *#CORPORATE CULTURE tweet Book01:* 140 Bite-Sized Ideas to Help You Create a High Performing, Values Aligned Workplace that Employees LOVE by S. Chris Edmonds

6. *#CORPORATE GOVERNANCE tweet Book01:* How Corporate Governance Adds Value to Your Business by Brad Beckstead

7. *#CROWDSOURCING tweet Book01:* 140 Bite-Sized Ideas to Leverage the Wisdom of the Crowd by Kiruba Shankar and Mitchell Levy

8. *#CULTURAL TRANSFORMATION tweet Book01:* Business Advice on Agility and Communication Across Cultures by Melissa Lamson

9. *#DEATHtweet Book01:* A Well-Lived Life through 140 Perspectives on Death and Its Teachings by Timothy Tosta

10. *#DEATH tweet Book02:* 140 Perspectives on Being a Supportive Witness to the End of Life by Timothy Tosta

11. *#DIVERSITYtweet Book01:* Embracing the Growing Diversity in Our World by Deepika Bajaj

THiNKaha® Learning/Training Programs Designed to Take You to the Next Level NOW!

THiNKaha® delivers high-quality, cost-effective continuous learning in easy-to-understand, worthwhile, and digestible chunks. Fifteen minutes with a THiNKaha® book will allow readers to have one or more "aha" moments. Spending less than two hours a month with a THiNKaha® Learning Program (either online or in person) will provide learners with an opportunity to truly digest the topic at hand and connect with gurus whose subject-matter expertise gives them an actionable roadmap to enhance their skills.

Offered online, on demand, and/or in person, these engaging programs feature gurus (ours and yours) on such relevant topics as Leadership, Management, Sales, Marketing, Work-Life Balance, Project Management, Social Media and Networking, Presentation Skills, and other topics of your choosing. The "learning" audience, whether it is clients, employees, or partners, can now experience high-quality learning that will enhance your brand value and empower your company as a thought leader. This program fits a real need where time and the high cost of developing custom content are no longer an option for every organization.

"This program has been very successful and in demand within Cisco. The vision and implementation of the THiNKaha Learning Program has enabled us to offer high-quality content both live and on-demand. Their gurus and experts are knowledgeable and very engaging."

- Bette Daoust, Ph.D
Former Learning and Development Manager, Cisco, and Internal Program Manager for THiNKaha Guru Series

Visit THiNKaha® Learning Program at http://thinkaha.com/learning.

Just **THiNK**…

- **C**ontinuous Employee/Client/Prospect Learning
- **O**ngoing Thought Leadership Development
- **N**otable Experts Presenting on Relevant Topics
- **T**ime Your Attendees Can Afford – 15 min. to 2 hrs/mo.
- **I**nformation Delivered in Digestible Chunks
- **N**ame the Topic—We Help You Provide Expert Best Practices
- **U**nderstand and Implement the Takeaways
- **I**nternal Expertise Shared Externally
- **T**raining/Prospecting Cost Decreases, Effectiveness Increases
- **Y**ou Win, They Win!